About the Book

Dixy Lee Ray grew up near the sea in Washington State. As a girl she set and met unique goals for herself. When she grew up, she earned a doctorate in marine biology and went on to become the first woman to head the Atomic Energy Commission and the first woman to be elected governor of the State of Washington.

The story of Dixy ·Lee Ray tells of a girl who developed an independence of mind and spirit that helped her become a nationally and internationally recognized leader.

an American Women in Science biography

Scientist and Governor,
Dixy Lee Ray

by Mary Ellen Verheyden-Hilliard

drawings by Marian Menzel

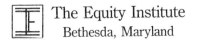

The Equity Institute
Bethesda, Maryland

This work was developed under a grant from the Women's Educational Equity Act Program, U.S. Department of Education. However, the content does not necessarily reflect the position of that Agency and no official endorsement of these materials should be inferred.

Fifth Printing 1997

Library of Congress Cataloging in Publication Data

Verheyden Hilliard, Mary Ellen.
Scientist and governor, Dixy Lee Ray.

(An American women in science biography)
Summary: Relates the story of Dixy Lee Ray, the first woman to be appointed head of the Atomic Energy Commission and the first woman elected governor of the state of Washington.

1. Ray, Dixy Lee—Juvenile literature. 2. Washington (State)—Governors—Biography—Juvenile literature. 3. Women scientists—United States—Biography—Juvenile literature. 4. U.S. Atomic Energy Commission—Officials and employees—Biography—Juvenile literature.
[1. Ray, Dixy Lee. 2. Women scientists. 3. Governors.
4. Washington (State)—Governors] I. Menzel, Marian, ill. II. Title. III. Series: Verheyden-Hilliard, Mary Ellen. American women in science biography.

Q143.R345V47 1985   509'.2'4 [B] [92]   84-25986
ISBN 0-932469-06-X

Scientist and Governor,
Dixy Lee Ray

"Governor! Governor Ray!" the reporter shouted. "How does it feel to be governor—the first woman elected governor of Washington?"

Governor Dixy Lee Ray smiled. The TV cameras were taking her picture. The crowd was cheering. Suddenly, time seemed to stand still.

Dixy remembered when she was 12 years old. She wanted to climb Mount Rainier, the highest mountain in America. She didn't know if she could do it. But she knew that if she didn't try, she'd never find out. Dixy did try, and she made it. Dixy was the youngest girl ever to climb all the way to the top.

Now she was the first woman to be governor of Washington. It seemed to Dixy she was still "climbing"—still trying to do things that were hard, and finding that she could do them.

Dixy Lee Ray was born on September 3, 1914, in Tacoma, Washington. She was the second of five daughters. Dixy's father had a very bad temper. His temper got worse when he drank too much. Then he would go get a stick. Dixy was hit many times with his stick. When things got too bad, Dixy went to the beach near her house. Dixy loved the water. She learned to swim in the sea.

She liked to watch the tiny fish near the rocks. Those fish are so small, she thought. They must eat something even smaller that I can't see. I wonder what it is that the fish can see, but I can't?

Dixy wanted to know all about everything that lived in water.

As she grew up, Dixy learned to make puppets. She and her sisters put on puppet shows about fairy tales. The shows were so good, people paid to see them. Dixy's mother drove Dixy and her sisters to schools, churches, and theaters where people waited to see the shows. Dixy liked earning her own money and feeling independent.

In high school Dixy joined the Debate Club and the Speakers' Club. She played in every sport open to girls. She won more medals in the swimming contests than anyone else. She also got an "A" in every class. Dixy's teachers told her she should plan to go to college.

Dixy's family did not have money for college. So Dixy had to plan how she would manage. First, her good grades helped her win a scholarship to pay part of the cost of college. Then, in college, she worked as a waitress, a telephone operator, and a janitor to pay the rest.

Dixy decided to study marine biology. "Marine" means the sea and "biology" means the study of living things. Dixy was still interested in everything that lived in water. After college, Dixy went to Stanford University and earned a doctorate. That is the highest degree a scientist can earn.

After college, Dixy became a teacher. She wanted girls and boys to learn about the things that live in water. She brought snakes and fish to school. She even brought a family of rats to class! The girls and boys loved her science class.

Dixy was asked to teach about science on TV. She caught water creatures and brought them to the TV studio to use on the show. People liked the way Dixy taught about science. Her series was a big hit.

Dixy was invited to take charge of the Pacific Science Center in Seattle, Washington. Her job was to make science interesting to everyone. Dixy got new exhibits. She said children could touch the exhibits and make them work. Thousands of people began coming to the Center because Dixy made science exciting.

Soon Dixy was chosen to be Chief Scientist on an important expedition. Scientists from all

over the world were to study the Indian Ocean while sailing on the *Te Vega*. *Te Vega* means "The Star."

When Dixy got to the *Te Vega*, she found it was filthy. Its engines didn't work. And the student helpers for the trip had decided they did not want to work very hard.

Dixy took charge. She fired the ship's captain and the ship's engineer. She hired others to run the ship. She convinced the students to do their job. When everything was ready, Dixy ordered the *Te Vega* to set sail.

The expedition was a success. Dixy had climbed another mountain.

The President of the United States asked Dixy to work on the Atomic Energy Commission. The Commission decided things about nuclear power for energy and nuclear power for weapons. Dixy thought these were very important decisions. She said she would take the job.

Dixy bought a big camper. She drove across America to her new job in Washington, D.C. Along the way, she visited atomic energy plants. She wanted to know what was happening with atomic energy in America.

After six months, the President asked Dixy to be head of the Atomic Energy Commission. She

was the first woman to hold that job.

Dixy decided to live in her camper while she was in Washington, D.C. She parked it in

a farmer's field just outside the city. She liked being in the country.

Every day a chauffeur drove up in a big black car. Dr. Dixy Lee Ray and her two dogs, Ghillie, a deerhound, and Jacques, a miniature poodle, got into the car. The chauffeur drove her to her office, where she was in charge of three *billion* dollars to be spent on atomic energy.

Dr. Ray sometimes smiled to herself at her memories. I scrubbed floors and waited on tables to pay for my college education, she thought. It certainly turned out to be worth it!

When Dixy left the Atomic Energy Commission, she decided to run for governor of Washington state. She talked to people all over the state. She spoke the truth as she saw it. The people elected her governor.

*   *   *   *   *

The woman in front of the microphones heard the reporter calling out again, "Is it going to be hard being the first woman to be governor of Washington?"

Governor Dixy Lee Ray smiled and waved to the crowd. She knew the answer. It was one more mountain to climb.

After she finished her term as governor, Dixy moved to Fox Island near Tacoma, Washington. Fox Island is a wilderness area of beaches and woodlands. Dixy's home is near the beach. She planted fruit trees all around her home.

Dixy has time now for fishing and wood carving. Her wood carvings are very beautiful. She also has time to write and talk with people who seek her advice.

Dixy has received dozens of awards from organizations, from magazines, from the U.S. Armed Forces, and from other countries. Twenty universities have awarded her honorary doctorates.

The United Nations awarded her the Peace Medal. The Kwakiutl American Indian Nation gave her their Certificate of Honor and named her "Oomah," which means "Great Lady."

Ever since she was a little girl Dr. Dixy Lee Ray has been willing to try new things and to work hard to achieve her goals. She thinks we all could achieve more in our own lives. Once, in a speech, she said:

"If...the honest, brilliant men and women among us prevail in this world, we can conquer anything—hunger, hate, pestilence, disease, war, fear. What is it we could not do?"

Also available from The Equity Institute:

You Can Be A Scientist, Too!
Companion video cassette to the
American Women in Science biographies.

Women: A Desk Reference
Highlighting 5,000 years of history
and 400 interesting lives.

For further information or a catalogue of
all Equity Institute publications, please write:

The Equity Institute, P.O. Box 30245
Bethesda, Maryland, 20814